Madgie

Madgie

A Life in Farming

MAJORY MACQUEEN

with additional material by

JANE MACAULAY

Librario

Published by

Librario Publishing Ltd.

ISBN: 978-1-909238-52-7

Copies can be ordered via the Internet
www.librario.com

or from:

Brough House, Milton Brodie, Kinloss
Moray IV36 2UA
Tel/Fax No 00 44 (0)1343 850 178

Printed and bound in the UK by Bell & Bain Ltd, Glasgow

Cover Design: Monika Gromek

Typeset by 3btype.com

Madgie with some of the Highland ponies she bred.
Picture by J.A. McCook

Foreword

By George C. Rafferty MBE DL,
retired veterinary surgeon, Grantown-on-Spey

Madge MacQueen was a Strathspey lass who dedicated her life to looking after the family farm, Achnahannet, high in the hills, with access by a track which was often blocked by snow in winter. She was an expert at handling animals including hill ponies, which were her speciality. No task on the farm was beyond her capability.

I first met Madge in about 1950, when I came to set up a veterinary practice in the area. I soon found she was not just a bonnie lass but could handle jobs such as castrating colts or assisting at difficult calvings with no problems. When the BBC made the TV series 'The Vet' in 1988–89, following me on my rounds which included visits to Madge's farm, she was quite the star. Even the professional producers admired her abilities.

Into her nineties she retained her wonderful memory and was consulted by the BBC and by Scottish universities. Visits to Achnahannet were always enjoyable and full of fun. We shall miss a remarkable lady.

Introduction

A stalwart of the farming community in Strathspey, Madgie MacQueen was familiar to anyone who attended the cattle mart in Grantown or the annual agricultural show, where she was equally at home selling calves, showing horses or exhibiting her home-produced butter and eggs. I had seen her there many times, particularly in the years when she was one of the show's organisers, as a prominent member of the Strathspey Farmers' Club.

In July 2015 my friend and neighbour Ailsa Black, who visited Madgie regularly, asked if I would like to become involved in helping to write down the old lady's memoirs. By this time she was 92 and becoming increasingly frail, but her brain was still sharp and full of memories.

So began a series of visits to the isolated farmhouse at Achnahannet, Madgie's lifelong home. About a mile out of Dulnain Bridge on the Carrbridge Road, a track turns off to the right and heads uphill for a couple of miles through a wooded area, past a scattering of houses and finally out on to the edge of the moor, with a magnificent view back down towards the Dulnain river and Strathspey. Madgie's ivy-clad traditional granite farmhouse, with its garden and outbuildings, seems to be at the end of the world and yet if you look further up the hill you can see the ruins of two more homesteads. When Madgie was a girl, there were people living in these houses and many more round about, for Achnahannet was part of a thriving community of people, all living off the land. In the summer, especially when the heather was in full bloom, the place looked like a paradise, and it was easy to see how she could want to spend her whole life there.

As we approached the back door, which was always unlocked and often wide open, I was aware of the gentle clucking of poultry. Hens, cockerels and chickens of various ages and stages scratched and wandered around, often walking in through the door to Madgie's kitchen, while wild rabbits grazed unafraid on the lawn. In the living-room sat Madgie, in front of her log-burning stove which she also used to cook her meals, surrounded by books, magazines, newspapers, letters, photographs and the general clutter of a busy life. And on another chair lay Peeping Tom, her elderly ginger cat who, like Madgie, had seen better days. Madgie's body was bent with arthritis and she relied on a walking frame to get around, but this didn't prevent her from going outside to feed her hens and collect the eggs each day. Her eyesight was also failing, which frustrated her as it became increasingly difficult to read and write. But her interest in all the comings and goings around her was as keen as ever and her memories were sharp, especially when it came to talking about her childhood and youth.

My original plan was to type up the many pieces of writing that Madgie had jotted down over the years and connect them with words of my own, but it soon became clear that she was a natural story-teller and that her life could only be told in her own words. So I placed a recording device in front of her, something which many people find intimidating. Not Madgie! She immediately leaned forward and went into performance mode. There were many interruptions, as the phone rang or other visitors arrived at the door. It was amazing how many people found their way to her remote farmhouse.

My last visit was in January 2016, when Madge boasted that so many people had come to see her over the New Year there were greater stocks of biscuits, cakes and bottles of Bailey's in her cupboard than there were in the general store in Dulnain Bridge. I was aware that she had become increasingly frail in the six months since I'd started visiting, but it was still a shock to receive a phone call a couple of weeks later to say that she had passed away. Apparently she had been feeling unwell in the afternoon and an ambulance was called. True to form, she was joking with the ambulance staff as they drove her away. She died that night in hospital.

Sad though it was, I can't help but be glad that she was able to be in her own home almost to the end as it's hard to imagine Madgie dragging out her days in a hospital or nursing home. I'm just pleased that I was privileged to be able to collect so many of her memories which might otherwise have died with her. It sounds like a cliché, but Madgie's death really is the end of an era. She was the last MacQueen to live and farm at Achnahannet and to experience a way of life long gone. And she was a true character, a one-off. We will not see her likes again.

Jane Macaulay

PART 1
Childhood

I was born on 22 June 1923 at Achnahannet, a small hill farm about three miles up in the hills behind Dulnain Bridge, and I still live there today, in the same house. You could say the furthest I've moved is from upstairs to downstairs. The road that goes up past the farm is one of the oldest in the area and goes right to Nairn, though it's hard to make out the track these days. Up past where our peat moss used to be there was a bit that was causayed (paved), so you could see that it was once a road. They must have taken the stones off the hill to do that. I've even heard that there was once a school there, up beyond Rynechra, which is the ruin you can see up on top of the hill.

I was the eldest of three sisters. Rita was born a year later, in 1924, and Betty in 1927. Rita and me were always together. Betty was younger, so was very spoilt, being the baby.

My father was the third generation to farm here. The family lived in another wee house at first, but they moved into this one in November 1894. My grandfather's diary lists the expenses for the new house, including two grates, a sideboard, three beds with mattresses, a meal chest, a washing stand, carpets and curtain, plus a plumber to lay 200 yards of lead piping and fit in a sink. That list came to £26, two shillings and eightpence.

The old boy, my grandfather, was a cattle dealer. He used to buy sheep and cattle all around locally and sell them as far afield as Yorkshire. In 1898 he bought a steam threshing mill and a traction engine to pull it. My grandfather and then my father took it round all the farms of Strathspey, from Cromdale and Grantown to Aviemore and Rothiemurchus, to thresh their corn. The engine came from McLean of Nairn and cost £149, while the threshing machine, which cost £100, came from John Thomson Alness and had to be transported by train at a cost of £2 10 shillings.

My mother came from Tomatin and the generation before that, her father, came from North Uist and the generation before that from St Kilda. They were one of the families removed at the end when they evacuated St Kilda. They had nothing in the food line left. I think they were just living on birds. Granny, my mother's mother, was born at Tombeg, up above Tomatin, above the railway. She married a Fraser who was in Drumbain and they stayed there until the old lady died. A great aunt, who lived to be one hundred and two, stayed in a cottage at the end of the steading. She always wore a long dress right down to her feet and a mutch (a close-fitting cap) on her head. The old lady died in that cottage too, but it's gone now and so is the house at Tombeg.

My mother could speak Gaelic and she could write it and if someone else that could speak it came in, the two of them would be laying off in Gaelic. But my father didn't speak it and neither did any of the folk in the crofts round about and none of us was interested in learning it.

We were never told how my mother came to meet my father. He was working on the roads at the time with the traction engine. The name of the firm was Shields and Ramsay. They were doing main road works, tarring the trunk roads. I think that's where they met because they were camped overnight. They had a sleeping wagon, a big wooden thing, and they used to sleep in that just below Drumbain House. And likely the women would be back and for visiting them. But we were never told the ins and outs of it all.

I once heard a story about my father and that traction engine. He was coming from Carrbridge back this way the day of the funeral of the old Dowager Countess of Seafield. She was to be buried in the church yard at Duthil. This man in a car – he was in advance of the rest of the funeral – going in the opposite direction to my father, stopped him and told him to get off the road because,

'I'm Lord Somebody-or-Other and I'm on very important business.' My father replied: 'I'm Dougald MacQueen and I'm on very important business too, so I'm going on home.'

My father was living on the farm of Gaich at the time, himself and his sister. Then when my grandfather died my father came back here, so this is where I was born. My father's brother was a banker in Grantown, the Bank of Scotland. His sister, she was called Madge, married a Sim, then their daughter, also called Madge, married one of the Milnes from Cromdale.

When we were growing up, there was always plenty to do on the farm. We kept fourteen cows, which were inside in the winter and out in the summer, and we had thirty sheep, always Blackfaces, which we clipped ourselves with the old hand shears. We used to like fine the clipping time and we all joined in. I used to go for the ones with bare necks, which were easier to do. We clipped the Clydesdale horses too and that had to be done in a straight line. Later on, when the fashion came in for wintering hoggs, we did that instead of keeping our own sheep. And we grew oats and turnips.

There was no hot water but we had a big boiler outside to which we carried the fire, several tubs and the old washing board. It was great fun for us to do the tramping of the blankets. A good windy day with some sunshine completed the job.

We had two milk cows. One calved in the spring: one in the autumn. Mother always did the milking, then she'd take the milk into the milk house, put it through a sieve and set it in basins. If we wanted curds, she would get out the rennet bottle and put a small drop in each bowl so that we could have curds and cream. The first basins she set were ready to have the cream lifted off and put into the cream jar, preparing for the butter. Eventually the cream was put into the big churn and we all had a go of turning the handle until the butter and the butter milk split. Then it was time to get out the big butter clappers and do your own shapes. If we had guests in the afternoon, the round butter balls were put on the table.

The dairy cow's calf was always fed out of a pail. He got to suck your fingers in the pail to start him off. Once he got the taste of the milk there was no stopping him but eventually he was able to get more solid food. As he got older, you just had to give a shout and he was there. When it was time to sell the calf, Mother always got the money for it and that almost covered the price of the groceries.

Mother made a lot of cheese too. We used to watch her working it all by hand and then it was wrapped in cheesecloth and taken out to the cheese press which was a big oblong stone. As the cheese was fermenting, the stone would be let down bit by bit. When it was ready it was all wrapped up again. My word it was good when we toasted a slice in front of the open fire and it was also very good with the oatcakes.

Mother always looked after the hens. When a hen got broody, she would set it on a dozen eggs. She always liked the Light Sussex hens and they were the best mothers. One day she got a new cockerel. He was shut in for two days until he got acquaint with the surroundings. When he got out he took off and the hens all ran down the field in front of him. The story goes that one hen then said to the other: 'We'd better slow down or he will miss us both!' As for that, I have yet to see a cockerel missing a hen! The hens were very useful for their eggs, as lots of baking went on. Scones, pancakes and oatcakes were the regulars.

Mother took eggs to the shop and they paid for the groceries. But we didn't need a lot of groceries – mostly bread and our father's tobacco. Our mother used to say to him: 'The dearest thing in the messages is your tobacco.' The shop we went to was MacLean's – Donald MacLean's shop, just at the end of this road. It was there when we were in school and if our mother was needing anything she'd ask us to get it at the shop on the way home. And if Mrs MacLean knew we were coming for the bread, she'd always take out a handful of sweeties for us. She was right good. Sometimes we would take down milk for her and leave it in a pail at the end of the road and when we got back the pail the next day, there would be a handful of sweeties in it. Donald MacLean also had a van and he went up the Skye of Curr road, though he didn't come up our road. But a horse and cart came from Remington's in Grantown on a Wednesday right up to our house. Our neighbour used to come here to buy loaves from the van. They made the round ones that were fashionable then.

You made your own cheese and butter of course and jam as well and there were always vegetables from the garden – carrots and cabbage, things like that. The only thing you'd find in a tin in those days was corned beef. You didn't get any of those other things. We bought the flour in bulk and it was kept in the meal chest: a great big wooden chest with a division in it. On this side was oatmeal: on that side was the flour. And the baking board and the utensils you used were in that as well. My Mother made scones and pancakes every other day – mostly griddle scones.

The old-fashioned table had a drawer in the end of it with all the knives and forks and when she was going to set the table, she just opened the drawer and everything was there. And always the tablecloth on. In fact I always used a tablecloth until maybe about ten years ago. I remember the household was getting less and less and Betty was getting married, I went into the drawer for the tablecloth and Rita said to me, 'What on earth are you taking that out for?' But it was part of my routine. My Mother always took off the tablecloth after dinner, in the middle of the day, and she always put on a clean overall in case anyone came visiting.

There was a tattie pit and a turnip pit and a swede pit. The swedes were always kept for the soup and the horses. The horses would get four swedes each in their boxes and they would always have to be cleaned. I remember my Father going with the hoe and scraping all the sand off them for the horses. After we had our dinner, in the middle of the day, it was time to let the cows out to drink from the burn. While they were out, we used to fill their hakes with straw and put a basket, or skull, of sliced turnips in each trough. The turnip hasher stood beside the pit and whenever we saw a slice we fancied we would eat it, there and then. They were really good, but the swedes were much sweeter than the yellow turnips. There was another kind of turnip slicer that was fixed to the cart wheel with a chain and you'd go out with that on the cart to feed the sheep. Nowadays all that has gone and the sheep are strip-grazed in the field where the turnips were grown.

Mother also made her own pot scrubbers. She would gather a bunch of heather just the length of her hand and wrist, then chop the ends off until it was even. Then she would take a strand of snare wire and wrap it round and pull tightly to make a good hand grip. She also made big brooms for brushing the causey in the byre and many other uses. There was no kitchen – just a milkhouse. We cooked on the range, which had big double ovens, in the living-room.

The toilet was in a shed outside, built of corrugated iron and many a row we got for throwing stones at this when there was someone in. The old toilet had a wooden seat which had to be scrubbed white and just a big pail. You'd to take your turn at emptying the pail. Then we got an Elsan closet. I used to fetch the container of stuff to pour into it. We didn't have inside plumbing until just before the war.

We got electricity in 1968. Television was the first thing we wanted then. Before that we had the wireless and you had to go and get your accumulator charged at the garage in Dulnain. You had to carry it on the bike and watch it didn't spill because it burned everything it touched. Then you'd go back a few days later to see if it was ready and often it wasn't ready because they'd forgotten to plug it in. If you had to buy a high tension battery it cost seven and six, which was dear then. You'd no radio until it was charged and of course you had no phone then either. Nowadays you wonder what you'd do without it.

The peat stack used to be out the back too. You cut your own peat, then you went up and set them up into hooacks, puckles all over the place. When you went to the moss you took your piece bag with you, with a couple of eggs and you hard-boiled them when you got there. There was a well not far from the moss and you got your wee fire going. The moss was away up at Clachbain there, where there's a flat piece of land but we took a short cut to get there. Everyone had their own peat moss. A lot of folk had their moss over at Clury, near where the wee shop, MacLean's, used to be. It's all trees now, but it was all peat moss then. The folk up the Finlarig road, that's where they got their peats. And then all the horses and carts, carting them home again, we came across them in the centre of the hill up there.

It was nearly all peat we burned, and the odd fir root that you dug up. They were good for kindling, for starting your fire. Once or twice we got the full length of a tree, where there had been a forest fire. Or maybe it was blown down by a gale or something – long, long ago. If you wanted wood for the fire you'd to buy it – I think it was about eight shillings for the tree. And the forester would go through, he would mark what you could take and you daren't take more than that number – your six or your eight or whatever – or you were in trouble. Once the forester had a lad working for him and they cut the tree and he got a handful of ground and was covering up the stump. The forester said: 'What on earth are you doing that for?' and he said: 'So folk will no' know that we're stealing.' He fairly put his foot in it!

There was a big garden with rhubarb, blackcurrants and all the vegetables. Mother always did the garden and the gate was high enough to keep us out. The bee hives were also kept in the garden. The honey was very good for colds or sore throats and Mother used it a lot in her baking. We always left enough to keep the bees going through the winter, then we would hap up the boxes to keep out the frost. We had eleven hives at one time and we used to sell some of it to the people who came during the shooting season.

When we took off the crates of honey the bees were not too happy. One time my sister got stung on the leg and it swelled up right away. When I was in town the grocer asked: 'Did you take off your honey yet?' I said, 'Oh yes, but my sister got stung on the leg and it's like a strainer post.' He said, 'Och, it doesn't matter. Her legs are like that anyway.' My sister was not impressed when I told her!

As a child, I always wanted to write but Mother would say: 'You haven't got the brains for that. You just like listening to old yarns.' Isn't it funny, when you were young you were told just to carry on with whatever you were doing, but the older generation always had visitors and the evenings were spent telling yarns, so I always kept my ear to the ground and listened to everything that was going on. That is how I gained my information, in those old tales.

Achnahannet was in the parish of Duthil and at that time the minister used to come round once a month and hold a service in one of the local farmhouses. So we all gathered at a neighbouring farm which was just across the field from us. We set off with our father to the service, all dressed up in our Sunday best. Strict instructions were laid down by our father that we would behave ourselves and 'no sniggering'. At the farmhouse we joined with the other worshippers from the glen and Mrs Grant welcomed us in. We all got seated and the Rev Peter MacGregor had his seat in the gable window. He welcomed everyone and took up his tuning fork and after a short prayer he started off the singing. My sister and I sat beside the box bed where our father could keep an eye on us. During the service a noise got up and all eyes and ears turned to the window where seven cows raced past. Last one in had forgotten to shut the gate! Mrs Grant gave a signal to Jock the farm servant to 'get them out of there' so Jock ran after the cows. Round and round the house they ran, followed by Jock and his dog. Each cow grabbed a mouthful of ivy or honeysuckle as it went and the dog's name changed several times from Gaelic to English. As the service went on, Mrs Grant went out herself to guide the cattle out the gate and Jock back into the service and a final cup of tea. Jock was furious to discover that one of the cows had skittered all over his Sunday best suit. Mrs Grant said, 'Jock, the Lord put up a good prayer for you.' Jock was not impressed and said, 'That's all very well, but it won't wash my suit!' 'Oh but we will put it out on the bleaching green,' said Mrs Grant. 'It's a good job there's not to be another service for a month.'

When we were older, more than twelve, we used to go to the church itself at Duthil. There was a shooting-brake that came from the Palace Hotel in Grantown and picked up the folk that were going to Duthil. When we were older still, we could cycle up the back road, past Mullochard, and there was a swing bridge that we used to walk across, taking the bike with us, and came out just at Duthil Church. We just went every second or third week. When we got there, we went into the church and your name was on the end of your pew. Our father always made us sit beside him so there would be no nonsense and no sniggering. That was one of the rules. The men were dressed in dark suits and the women in dark costumes but everyone wore a hat. A lot of people used to come from the Boat of Garten side of the parish, walking all the way across the hill and out at Mullochard. They crossed the River Dulnain by the swing bridge. Now the bridge is washed away and the church has been taken over by the Clan Grant society.

When the churches of Duthil and Dulnain combined, we didn't go to church for years. We thought folk would be speaking about us, coming from Duthil. There's a poem about the Men of Duthil who were supposed to be wicked men, causing trouble wherever they went. It was silly, but that was in our minds. (Actually the 'Men of Duthil' usually refers to a particularly strict Presbyterian sect who worshipped in the woods at Duthil after the Disruption of the Church of Scotland in 1843 and before the Free Church was built in 1850). But the minister always came up here to visit us and our mother did the collecting for the church.

From the age of five, we went to school at Dulnain Bridge three miles away, walking all the way there and back. There were two routes. In winter we walked right down the Achnahannet track to the main road and along it to the village, but in summer we took what was known as 'the scholars' path' across to Balnuichk and over the hill, coming out at the back of the village. Sometimes we had races, with some of us taking one way and some of us the other way. They took more-or-less the same time. On 'the scholars' path' you had a bit of climbing but you made up for that by going fast down the other side. We had our playtime piece with us, which was two slices of bread for dinner time, with jam or very often crowdie or cheese, and pancakes and scones for the mid-morning and afternoon breaks. And if we came home by Balnuichk, Mrs McLennan would give us a pancake with blackcurrant jam. We were lucky. There was a big stove in the school, surrounded by a fine big heavy guard and we were allowed to dry our wet clothes on it on rainy days. At midday in the winter we were allowed a cup of cocoa which was handed out by the older girls.

There were about sixty pupils in the school in the three rooms. There were three teachers – Mr McKinnon the headmaster, Miss Carr, who cycled all the way from Nethy every day and she always had a bottle of Camp coffee, and Miss Forbes – she lodged in Dulnain.

There was quite a crowd of us walking home together. The farm workers at Tullochgribban, they all had big families you see, and the ones at Balnaan and Muckrach, the whole way down the road. And all the way up this road, but we were the farthest. And coming home from school we could do as much damage as anyone else. I wasn't one of those that broke the wee white caps on the telephone lines, throwing stones at them. You had to have a good aim to hit them. I got blamed for it but it wasn't me.

There was one boy in particular, a spoilt brat, he was the only one of us who owned a bike and he used to go in and out of us with the bike to try and knock you off balance and grab the bag off your back. I said to Rita: 'He'll not do it tomorrow,' and she said: 'He'll do it, same as every other blooming day.' Never mind! Down at the end of the road there was a lot of broom there. I picked up a dead stick, a long stick, and when he came along the road I put it right through the spokes of his wheel and of course down he went, howling and crying. The next day we set off down to the school and before we reached the end of the road we saw him going along the road on the bike and Rita said: 'I bet he's away down to the school to report you' and I said: 'Surely not!' So straight into the school I went and McKinnon says: 'Marjory MacQueen. Hold out your hand!' He took the strap out of the desk, then 'boom'. 'Do you know what that's for?' I never opened my mouth. He said: 'You have no right to knock a boy off his bike. That's what that's for and don't you dare do it again.' I was near bubbling by then, back into my seat. I sat beside Topsy Calder from Nethy and she said: 'I'd have done the same and more!' So I didn't regret it one bit.

Rita got sewing at school but I never did. I think I had dictation or something instead. If you passed such-and-such an exam, you didn't get the sewing. At one time we were all knitting scarves and I always remember Ella Grant from Balnaan walking up the road from Dulnain towards Muckrach Lodge and the ball of wool fell out of her bag but of course nobody said anything about it. We sniggered about it but never let on and walked on and on and on and the knitting was all dirty by then. I should have told her, but there you are. She said, 'You are wicked.' Wicked. But that's how kids can be.

But I liked the schooldays all right. I got on quite well. There used to be the girls' playground and the boys' playground and the same with the toilets – and the fights used to be in the middle one.

One of the older boys arrived at the school one day very excited: 'Please miss, I have a baby sister.' The teacher said, 'Oh how nice, and what are you going to call her?' He answered 'Bessie Bummer.' 'What a strange name! Who is she called after?' 'One of the black cows at

Ballintomb.' That was a very popular herd in those days. So poor Bessie remained Bessie Bummer all her days.

If it was a stormy winter, we stayed in lodgings up at Duthil, at that house beside the church, Seafield it was called, with Mrs Rose, and we'd go to school at Duthil because it was nearer than trying to go from here to Dulnain. You weren't allowed to stop out of school. You had to go to school.

At the start of the summer holidays, the two top classes in Dulnain School used to walk to the dairy farm of Tullochgorum for strawberries and cream. What a treat! They had their own cream, but they bought in the strawberries.

There was plenty to do in the holidays. When we were little, we would go for walks, but always within sight of the house. One thing we would do was see who would make the longest daisy chain and bring it back to the house without it breaking. Another day would be spent at the burn side watching the minnows darting to and fro, always trying to catch one in a jam jar but we never succeeded. Next ploy was to stop at the rushes and make baskets. Once we got into the knack of pleats and winding them round in small circles, we were able to make various sizes of baskets. The harder job was to make handles without breaking the stem and winding the sharp point into the main basket. And there were plenty of picnics with home-made cakes and bottles of milk.

Sometimes we would go to play at Balnuichk and the great thing there was an absolutely super swing with chains in a giant larch tree. I was driven past there the other day and the tree had been struck by lightning right through the top. It was a huge tree. I don't know how many circles would be in it. I thought to myself: That's another landmark gone.

As we got older, we were always busy helping out with tasks on the farm. In the spring we had to go to the barn and put the oats through the fanners so that they would be nice and clean for sowing. The sowing was done by hand with a sowing sheet.

Next job was to hoe the turnips, so the horses were yoked to the drill harrow which cleaned the drills and made the hoeing much easier. A neighbour came to give us a hand with the hoe, which was the done thing. Our mother brought down the tea to the field, so they all sat down enjoying their tea and putting the world to rights while Rita and I counted the studs on the men's boots. Tea finished, we went home, leaving the two men in a cloud of tobacco smoke.

Once the hoe was finished, we went to the peat moss to set up the peats to dry off. We took advantage of the dry weather to cut the hay. We loved the smell of the clover and so did the bees. Nowadays there is not nearly as much clover in the grass seed mixture. Once it was dry enough the horse was yoked into the rake and the hay gathered into rows ready for setting up into coles (small mounds) and left to dry out. Next it was all carted home to the stack yard and built into stacks for the winter, all roped down and secure from gales.

The corn was cut in the autumn and tied into sheaves which we had to set up in stooks, all facing in the same direction so the prevailing wind would dry it out. As time went on, the binder came into fashion, although there was not much room for it on the small fields of the crofts. The binder twine made a very tidy job of the sheaves, but as the crop was set up in stooks the grouse moved in and helped themselves to the oats.

I remember leading (taking in corn to the stack, once it had dried in the stooks) and old Bob the Clydesdale, if he had a chance he'd take a mouthful out of the corn and my father would be: 'Hey, get that horse out of that!' Messing up the stook, you'd get a row for that. 'Go on. Tidy it up yourself.' You had to pull out a few straws and tie them up and make a knot. You'd do it by hand then, before the days of the binder. And of course, if it was the harvest you were going to you'd to put the harvest frame on to the cart

– a big wooden frame so you could take bigger loads. And you had to build them properly. And when you were forking into the stack you had to do it the right way. There was a right way for everything.

Once the harvest was finished, we used to thatch the stack with rashes and tie them up tightly in case they would get pelted with the gales. There was an art to building a corn stack. Every sheaf had to be put in exactly the right place. Then when you were finished someone would go round with a spade and knock in any sheaves that were sticking out at all. That kept it neat and watertight. And when you were making your stacks you had to make a 'bothy' in the stack with a wooden frame, to let the air through. The hens used to creep in there and make their nests. They still do sneaky things like that.

Old-fashioned farming had its compensations. Walking behind a pair of horses you would spot all the birds' nests and stones of many colours, but sitting on a tractor you miss all those interesting things. With all the modern machinery, fewer men need to be employed, which means more cash to spend on implements.

I always liked the horses. You did everything with them. We had two Clydesdales and a Highland pony, called Tommy. The horses were called Bob and Nell. And then there was the old war horse. The time of the

1914–18 war, the military went round all the farms and collected the horses. And if you gave them one, they stamped its hoof, stamped for the Army, and when the horses came back at the end of the war you got the chance of one to make up for it. You had to go to a pick-up point. I can't remember where that was. So we got old Dod and we had him till he died.

Another thing I remember. When we were going to school one day there was this great big cart and a big Clydesdale pulling it and a horse standing in the cart. That was the stallion doing his rounds of the farms. He had to be carried in the cart to rest him. We couldn't wait to get home to tell what we saw: a stallion standing in a cart. Good gracious!

From the age of about fourteen or fifteen you learned how to put on the harness. The two horses were side by side, the two big ones, and the saddle was hanging up the back of the stable and the collar was on a different hook. I'm quite sure the horses knew fine and they'd be saying to themselves: 'I wonder is she taking down the saddle or the back band?' You see it would be the saddle for the cart but for anything else, the plough or the harrows, it would be the back band, the one that takes the chains. Our father taught us how to put on the collar. You turned it upside down and then the horse poked his head in.

We had a young horse that we broke in by putting him on the harrows. The first time I had them out as a pair in the field, I was turning them up at the top of the field while my father was fencing. I got them all entangled – their feet entangled in the chains. My father said: 'You got them into that mess. You get them out of it.' What a job I had! 'Will I louse off the chain and put his feet over or what?' He says: 'You put them in there. Get them out of there.' Which I did in the end, no bother at all. I hadn't been keeping the left rein tight enough.

The Highland pony had a wee cart himself. An Irishman made it and put ribbons on it. There's a photograph of him and the other horse out in the snow, making tracks for the sheep to take them up into the wood for shelter.

I remember setting off in the early morning to get the mare shod at the smiddy in Grantown. The horse knew every stop. At Craggan she would hurry to get a drink from the burn, then on to the smiddy and the noise of the hammers on the anvil. A good fire would be roaring and the bellows pumped up to heat the iron. The blacksmith would measure the feet and bring down the correct size of shoes. Both men wore leather aprons and had their nails in wooden trays beside them. Sparks would be flying from the red hot iron as the shoe was fitted and all the surplus hoof rasped off. During this time, we had all the news of the town! Once the job was done and the hoofs polished up with oil, we set off again for the seven-mile ride home. I remember stopping at Duncan's the baker's because I was getting hungry. The horse waited outside the shop while I went in and got a pie. Then I climbed on to the window sill and on to the horse's back and off again. Imagine trying to do that today! Then you could stop and have a blether with the local cyclists heading into town and you got a wave from the workers in the fields. As time went on, the blacksmith got a trailer for his car and travelled out to the farms with all his equipment.

We had horses right up to the 1940s, just after the war. The last one died on the farm, but he was idle for about a year and a half before that. Any horse that died here was buried here and that was some job, digging a hole with a spade. There's a mound round the back of the brae there and it's called the Torran and there was an old cow that died the same day as the horse. The two of them are buried on that mound.

Our father had a tractor before the war, an old Fordson, they were the ones with the cleats in the wheels, the next one was the 'splayed lugs', to give you a grip. They were all metal wheels – no rubber tyres in those days. The old Fordson tractor, it had to go with the fourth turn of the handle. If not, they said, the air would turn blue! So there were some things that you did with the horse and some things that you did with the tractor. The tractor was no use for planting turnips, as it would make too much of a mess turning at the end. You'd get a row if the wheels of your cart went over the turnips. When you turned your horse you'd turn it in between the dreels – 'not on the top of the neeps!' You got all those sort of rows but you soon got used to it.

I started driving with those old tractors, but I don't remember when I started driving a car. I think about seventeen. I had a truck, it was red and black, an Austin A70. When people saw it they would say: 'Here comes the fire engine!'

When you'd gathered all the crops in, then you started emptying the midden to be ready for the next lot of dung from the byre and if it was a frosty morning it would be grand to stand in the midden because your feet would be warm. Everything was done by hand, with the graip, (a curved fork) and it was graiped out at the other end. You didn't put the end gate on to the cart if you were to be turning it out onto the stubble because you had a thing like a hook and you just stood at the back and pulled it out every five or six yards or so and you got a row if it wasn't right in line. Like the stooking, you had to keep them straight in line and all facing the same direction to let the wind through. Everything had to be done in line.

We had time for fun too. Our father played the accordion and the violin and people would come round to the house for entertainment. Oh aye, we had a lot of good nights at home. We had lots of visitors. Even though you'd think it's far away, when it comes to a night like that, it's not far away. And there were a lot of singers too in those days – a lot of local folk who could sing. We had a piano too. I never learned to play myself. There was someone doing classes in Grantown but it was so far to go back there after school. And all the jobs to do when you got home. You'd even have to walk up the burn to see there was no hoggs drowned in it. The hoggs were wintered and you wanted to return them all in the spring. You just got paid for those that went back.

In the summer we took in visitors. You put a bit in the paper, saying how much it was, and you'd get replies. Sometimes the same people would come back year after year if they liked the area. While we were children, several rooms were added on at the end of the house, but they were pulled down again later because they were starting to go. We stayed in that part and the visitors had this part and my mother would cook for them.

When we were young, we often used to see the travelling

Achnahannet – surrounded by heather in bloom.

Annual hare shoot party.

Rita and Betty on a pony while Madgie holds its head.

Rita with a Clydesdale and Madgie with a Highland pony.

Madgie building stooks of corn.

Madgie's mother Elizabeth, carrying jugs of tea to the workers.

Madgie as president of Strathspey Farmers' Club in 1989, crowning the beauty queen at the Grantown Show.

*All dressed up – the three sisters and their Mother,
in front of the farmhouse.*

Betty, Rita and Madgie with a calf.

Driving one of the old tractors.

Showing off some perfectly built corn stacks.

A binder at work.

Building a hay stack.

Grandfather and Father, both called Dougald, wearing the same tartan but at different times.

Corn stacks in the snow.

Pictured in Dulnain Bridge – the steam threshing mill and traction engine which Madgie's Grandfather and Father took around the farms.

*The three sisters – Betty, Rita and Madgie – pictured at the
front door of their farmhouse.*

people, known to us as the 'tinkers', on their rounds with the pony and cart, selling their wares which included brushes, combs, safety pins, hairnets and clothes pegs, also mugs, plates and cups of various designs. They also sold butter clappers and thistles carved out of wood and pot scrubbers made from the heather, as well as pails, enamel basins and home-made tin basins, brushes and doormats. They would ask for any rabbit skins, which were always kept for them anyway. The rabbit was skinned right from the tail out over the head, then the skin was hung to dry. Springtime brought the women selling 'Kessock herring' – they were small but very good. The tinkers would usually travel as a family. They would split up and each one would take a basket of stuff to sell. They never left without getting a few eggs and a wisp of straw for their horse.

A lot of these people were very musical. We would see them standing at the roadside playing the pipes or the accordion. The bonnet lay at their feet, always hoping that someone would drop in a coin. The travelling people appeared to have quite a happy way of life.

Back at the farm, one of the jobs we had as children was training the calves to walk with us on the halter, as the heifer calves had to be trained if they were to be kept for breeding. Only the bigger farms kept a bull, so the cows had to be led to the nearest one. On one occasion this man set off with his cow to the bull, but the cow was terrible thrawn on the rope. When he got there, he was told a yarn about a previous cattleman who was on his way to the farm when he stopped to open a gate. The cow jumped on his back and its front feet landed in his pockets – so he just carried on, carrying the cow on his back! What an imagination… or what a yarn!

Once the animals were in for the winter, it was time to book the threshing mill. It meant a lot of extra cooking. A huge pot of potatoes was peeled and cooked and a big piece of beef was boiled to make broth. Extra tables were set and the big tablecloths taken out. The threshing brought the neighbouring farmers to help. They would be served the broth, followed by the beef, along with the potatoes, mashed together with turnip, served on great ashets.

We ordered 'railway bags' to fill with oats if we were selling any. The rest was carried up to the loft. A traveller used to come round and take a sample of the oats with him, then he would phone and quote a price per quarter. The railway bags were very heavy but very strong. You had to pay for hiring them. Ones that were torn were sent to the prisons for repair.

When the mill went away, we sent some oats down to Father's cousin for her hens. Ann was in town when we got there, but had left out her washing to dry. Temptation got the better of us and we stuffed her bloomers with straw (present-day pants are so small, you could fill them with a handful of chaff!)

I heard of a woman who crofted on the Dava Moor and she had a 'tinny' – a small thresher that had to be pedalled by foot fast enough to thresh the oats. Of course the crop was all cut with the scythe and bands of straw were made to keep each sheaf together. The bigger the sheaf the harder the old lady's legs had to pedal, which amused the boys who were helping.

Afterwards we'd take the corn to the mill at Mullenfenachan or to the mill up at Duthil or to Mrs MacLennan at Craggan. There was a choice of mills and they were all quite good. You'd take in so many bushels of oats. You'd a round roller like one of those old curtain poles and you rolled it across the top of your bushel to make it flat, so you had the correct amount in your bushel. You put it through the fanners – the old barn fanners which was made by Anderson's in Grantown. Our father would be turning the handle and we'd have to take turn about to hold the pail. There were three different spouts. Chaff went straight into the chaff house and then one spout was for your lights, one was for seconds and the other one was for the best grain, so you pulled out this tray to see which one you wanted. The best stuff went for oatmeal or for sowing and the seconds went to the hens. A lot of the oats went for bruising to feed to the cattle. The bruiser out here was worked by a pulley from the tractor.

If there was a cow calving, you'd to take the stable lantern and go out to the byre. We took turns Rita and me – Betty never had to go. It would be great if, as soon as you got to the gate there, you heard this low 'moo'. Then you'd know she'd calved so you'd go back into the house and mix up a handful of oatmeal with some water and take it back out to the cow. You'd see her licking the calf and that would be great. You hated it if you went out and there was no sign of a calf yet and you'd to go back and fro for the rest of the night. I can hear that low 'moo' yet. The cows knew fine what they were getting, if they saw you coming with the pail,

In our summer holidays we used to go to Tomatin most years, to stay with our grandparents – just the two of us, Rita and me, until we were about twelve. After we were twelve you'd to start doing jobs at home. It wasn't a case of running out and playing all the time, unless our mother was having visitors and we weren't included in the conversation. Then it was: Go away and play!

We used to stay with the grandparents for a fortnight. We were picked up here and taken down with the grocer's van. Jimmy Cumming was his name – he'd the shop at Carrbridge. That was great excitement getting down in the van, and we'd get back with him as well. Another time we got down with the lad that was the gamekeeper. How did we spend our time there? Well, there was a topping swing, just up behind the house. We spent a lot of time there. Other times we would walk up to the railway line and collect coal. Whoever was the fireman on the train at the time, he'd throw off a shovel of coal and blow a whistle so we'd know to collect it. And then we would walk from there, right through what they called the Green Road, down to Drumbeg School. Now the road's all houses. That big viaduct you see off the road – you go under that. We spent a lot of time on that road. We'd go right down and come up the back of the manse and out on the main road again. Very often Auntie Maggie would come with us. We got lots of rows from her. We got plenty of rows altogether. She'd say: 'Stop that! Lift your feet properly, like horses. Don't wear out the studs on your boots'. If she said 'Bring in the sticks' or 'Bring in the coal' you'd to do it right away and that was that.

At the fireplace, there was a big stove with a boiler at the end and the old grandfather was continually boiling sheep's horns in there to soften them for walking sticks, and then he would twist them into whatever shapes. He had a wee workshop with wee vices and tiny little files. Many's a day we would try to get at them but no – he always had his key in his pocket. That was his quarters so you never got to play in there.

And then, when it was time, you'd to go and take the cows home or put them back to another field. All those kind of jobs and Aunt Maggie was very, very strict. So anyway, they're all gone – all gone except old MacQueen here!

Sometimes we used to go down to the grocer at the big iron bridge. Or we'd go down to the end of the road and sit beside the sheep's fank and see how many cars we would see on the A9. One day we went down for the day and took a picnic and we saw four cars. Big excitement! We went home to tell them we saw four cars the whole day. But we saw so many on their bikes.

And then other times we use to go up to Molly Fisher's at Slochd which was a tearoom. They had a picture on the wall of an elephant walking along the road there. Apparently when the circus was on its way to Inverness, with the animals in the vans, they'd stop at the Slochd to give them some exercise so that's when the picture was taken. We'd have our tea there, then walk back on the old, old A9 which went along through the centre of the hill, and back down to Drumbain. There were cottages along the roadside then.

On Sundays the church service was held in the birch wood in an elevated position above the old A9 road looking towards the River Findhorn. The wooden seats were placed in rows among the birch trees. Before the service we had to go there armed with pails and shovels and clean up the grass where the cows had slept the night before. On returning to the house we sat in silence and listened to the singing. No organ, just one man in full voice led the way, while the curlew and oyster catcher kept to their own tune.

I got out of school to help with the harvest – I'd have been about eleven – and I'd just been back a week when my mother sent a letter to the schoolmaster to see if I could get off school again so that I could go and visit the cousins in North Uist. And I got off no bother at all. I think if you were kind of clever you did get off, but if you were a dunce you wouldn't because they thought you were no' learning. The schoolmaster McKinnon came from Portree, Skye, and he was quite good to the West Coast folk. There used to be quite a few folk would say: 'How did she get off and other folk didn't?'

So when we went out to the islands the bobby, they called him Harris Tweed because he came from Harris, met us at the boat, the *Loch Seaforth* I think was the name of it. And this woman was carrying a hamper and he shouted at her to leave it and he would carry it because the stones were slippery going up from the pier on to the road. So he carried the box and he said: 'What have you got here?' Oh, she said, it was a cockerel, she was carrying it out to her sister. So off she went with it. When we came back at the end of the fortnight, here was the wifie coming back on the boat still carrying the hamper. 'Good gracious,' says the bobby, 'you're back with that hamper again.' 'Oh yes,' she says, 'there's no way would I leave the cockerel with thon brutes of hens she has. They would have killed him. I'm taking him back home'.

We stayed with an old relative in a black house, the sort that was thatched and you had to go through the house to get to the byre. Years later I remembered that old house and made a model of it and a few others like it. I remember one of the houses just had flagstones on the floor and every morning the woman would scatter them with fresh sand from the seaside and use a besom to sweep the old stuff out and new stuff in.

We didn't celebrate Christmas very much but we did have Santa Claus. Our stockings would be hung up in front of the fire. You'd get an apple and an orange in it and sweeties and as you got older it was clothes that was in it – pants or something like that. The folk from up the road at Rynechra, Nan and her mother, were always invited down for their Christmas dinner. We'd usually have a chicken but we had turkey once or twice – home-reared. And you'd get a threepence or a sixpence rolled up in paper inside your pudding – your clootie dumpling. It was a great big clootie dumpling. You'd put up decorations across the ceiling, but you'd be careful to keep them away from the Tilley lamp.

New Year was a bigger thing. You'd to be home before midnight to take in Hogmanay at home. So everyone arrived and when the clock struck twelve everyone went out the door, shook hands and wished everybody a good New Year. Then when we got back in, Mother produced all the drams, the black bun and the plum pudding and the cake and shortbread galore and everybody helped themselves. Then they would go to visit the neighbours. If there was a man with black hair, they always pushed him into the house first because he was supposed to be the one that brought the luck. And then the toast – you'd haud up the dram and say: 'Here's tae us, wha's like us? Damn few and they're a' deid,' and the other one was 'Lang may your lum reek wi' other folk's coal.' We'd just go to the near neighbours, but when we got older we'd go away on the bike, over to Balnaan and Gallovie. People would come to you the next day – the next few days in fact. Once or twice we'd have someone staying overnight because they weren't fit to go home. I remember it was a very dark stormy night one year and several people came up, so they stayed all night. We saw them off the next day, after opening the road with the horse plough.

We always fired a gun at midnight, at twelve on the dot. The last time I did that was about twenty years ago. Father always did it before that, but our mother wouldn't handle a gun, not at all. My gun was a short one. It had its own box to keep it in, probably made by pupils in the school. But when they changed the laws on gun ownership in 1997 I'd to hand it in, which I did, so that was the last time I fired a gun at New Year.

PART 2

Growing Up

When primary school came to an end, anyone with a few brains won the Donald Smith memorial prize, five or six big heavy books. What a job it was humping all those books up here to the farm! *The History of Mankind* was one of the books and one about Canada. They were good books, but way beyond my knowledge at that time. I passed some of them on to Sandy Gordon, Angus Gordon's brother, when he was going away to college or university or whatever.

Once we were twelve we had to go to secondary school in Grantown, seven miles away. There was a test to see if you were fit to go to Grantown and if not you'd to stay another year at Dulnain. Because we were more than three miles from the school, we got a bike from the county. I remember the make – it was an Ellswick. They were supposed to be good bikes then, so they likely were. I've still got it, hanging out in the shed. Once when we left school at the end of the day we all got together, the people from Dulnain and Nethy, and decided to cycle to everyone's home, into Nethy and back by Clury. Big mistake. We didn't realise just how long it would take. We were in trouble when we got home late – but we were always in trouble anyway! The next time the Nethy folk were to come to Dulnain, but it was so far, we never did it again.

I liked Grantown school right enough, but I was just there until I was fourteen. By that time our father was starting to get disabled with arthritis and he was in bed for about fourteen years. So that left Mother and us girls to do all the work of the farm. I got a leaving certificate from the school and then, after I left, I went to evening classes. There were three of them – poultry, bee-keeping and the Red Cross, all in the hall in Dulnain. I have certificates for those three things.

My father died in 1955. There was a terrible storm and the road was blocked. The County opened it the night before. Men came from Kingussie and opened up the road with spades, but there was a blizzard that night and the whole thing was blocked again.

In 1957 an RAF aeroplane crashed on top of that hill. It was the day of the threshing mill at Muckrach. We heard an awful bang and someone came down the road and said: 'There's an aeroplane crashed at the back of the house, just on top of the hill there.' My Mother phoned the police and the Air Force guys came up. There was just one person, the pilot, and he was killed. There were people back and forth for weeks, trailing bits of that aeroplane, but there are still bits up there.

The Cattle Show in Grantown was always a highlight. The morning of the Cattle Show, we had two horses entered. I had the Highland pony and Rita had one of the Clydesdales and we had to leave at quarter past six to get there, on horseback, in time for the judging. It rained all day and we were soaked. Then we had to ride them back home. There was no word of horseboxes then. When we got back home after the show, we had our jobs to do and then our supper and a rest and then back in for the dance at night, on the bike this time – but it was dumped at the roadside once or twice on the way home! That was it. That was the kind of entertainment they had in those days.

We used to go off to anything we could go to – all the dances of the day. We always had energy to get there and get back and play tricks on other folk. One time we were cycling home from a dance and one of our friends said she wasn't coming home with us, she was going home with a young man. So we got so far when we recognised her bike, leaning against a haystack. We decided to play a trick on her, so we tied her bike to one end of the rope that went over the stack. Then we got the other end and pulled, so the bike was up high in the stack and we left it there. Much later, the girl came in by our house on her way home and she was shouting for our mother, so she could tell her what a pair of 'bad bitches' her daughters were.

What a rage she was in! Of course our mother knew nothing about it, so we had to do all the explaining the next day.

At the threshing mill, Rita and I were carrying the sacks up to the loft and there was this lad helping. Rita threw a 56 lb weight into one of the bags he was carrying and he was struggling with it up the stairs and when he got round to emptying the bag... Oh what a row she got! So she never did that a second time.

One evening Rita and I went visiting the gamekeeper's house at Balnouchk. When we were passing the clothes line at the back of the house, we saw all the long johns hanging on it and we thought: let's tie each leg to another one, which we did. At half past eight the men went out to feed the horses and the bull. When they came back in, they were saying: 'What a cold frosty night! Rita looked at me, I looked at her and we both thought about the washing. After the tea I said, 'We'd better go,' and Bessie said, 'I'll walk you to the end of the wood.' I said, 'Not at all. We can go on our own,' but she said, 'I usually do it and I'll do it this time too.' We went out of the house, within sight of the washing-line and we could see this solid mass of washing. So we were saying. 'What's that Bessie, away over there?' until we got past it, 'And over there that's the Boat and that's Nethy and you can see right the way to Carrbridge.' By this time we were up at the end of the wood and persuaded Bessie not to come further. We could hardly get home for giggling and laughing. Next day the gamekeeper arrived down and we were out at the tattie pit – I can see him yet. 'Is your mother in?' 'Oh yes, she's still in bed I think.' 'Oh well, I'm going in. I've something to tell her.' So he went in and he said to our mother: 'By go, that two dames of yours are in trouble!' Of course she was that taken aback, she didn't know what to say.

Rita and I used to go off on cycle rides all over the place at the weekend, with something to eat in our pocket, and sometimes we went off with the horses, away up in the hills.

At different times we had all sorts of animals. We had two donkeys and a goat – an old billy goat. Once he got out and went right over to Balnouchk. They had a bit fenced off for swedes, to keep the sheep out, but he went and he climbed over the fence and ate the swedes. And he also went into Mrs Whiteford's garden and ate some fancy trees that she planted. So the postman came round here and he said, 'By gosh, you're in for it.' And I said, 'What's wrong?' He said, 'Your goat's eaten Mrs Whiteford's trees.' So of course, nothing for it but to go up and get him. They'd caught the goat and shut him in but the goat heard my voice and started bellowing as if to say: 'Let me out, I'm shut in here.' So I said: 'Let him out and he'll come home with me.' Which he did, no bother. There was a stile on the fence up there, the march fence. He saw me on the stile and he just did the same thing. Up and over the fence and all the way home.

Then we had geese. Someone visited and wanted some geese and I said 'Take some of mine. Take two geese and a gander.' So he went off with them, away round the other side of the hill in the Landrover. Soon afterwards, Mother was looking up the road and she said, 'Hey. Come and see this.' And here's the geese coming walking home. They'd walked all the way around the hill until they got to the cattle grid, but they couldn't get across that. So I went off to the grid, over on the bike, and I managed to get them across. I had a stick, put the stick lying down, and they crossed between the fence and the stick.

We even had a wildcat once. The keeper found it stuck in a wreath of snow at Duthil, at the roadside. He just picked it out of the snow and put it in his pocket and brought it here – just a wee, wee kitten. We kept it in here in a cage and tried to get it tame. And after a while I said to Rita one night: 'Put the cage opposite the TV so that it can see folk moving about.' So we did and it worked wonders. But it was never really tame. If you put food down to it, it would just bite your fingers right away. So anyway, one night we decided to try it outside. For a while it stayed around and would come in for food, but one day it just took off and never came back.

There was always plenty of entertainment in those days and we went to every concert that was in the area. Sandy Cameron had a gramophone and he used to take it to Dulnain Hall for concerts. I remember we came home late one night and my mother said, 'What on earth kept you?' and Rita just said, 'Oh well we were waylaid on the road.' Oh yes – the good old days. The women always wore skirts then. There was no word of trousers till the war. When the trousers came in they were the best things out.

Then we used to go off poaching at night, when the fish were coming up the river in October. I remember Rita saying: 'I'm sure I heard a splash in the burn tonight.' And right enough, we got the gaff and the bag and the whole caboodle and way down to the Leantach Burn and by gosh, we got all these fish. Mrs Macaulay stayed in the Mill and her son Billy had just been made the new water baillie. Rita says to me: 'What's that light that keeps going off and on?' It was the water baillie walking along the burn shining his torch and we had all these fish in the bag and the gaff and all, so we lay flat in the bog myrtle. We were soaked to the skin, but not a squeak – we never spoke or anything. And the light passed and passed and back again and at last it went away. So we said: 'That's us. Better get going,' so we cut up to the road. And blow me, instead of going back along the burn, the baillie went back by the road. So sure enough we had to get off the road again. The next day Mrs Macaulay was on the phone and our mother said to her: 'How does Billy like the new job?' She said, 'It's fine but there's someone getting fish already.' My Mother says, 'Surely not.' 'Oh yes' she says, 'There were fish in the burn. He knows where the beds were and they're gone.' So they never guessed and the funny thing was, we were always good friends with the family. But we never felt guilty – no, not a bit.

We were great on going ferreting too. We had four ferrets at a time as a rule. We had more at one time but our father said: 'No, you're not keeping any more.' We'd put up our ferreting nets and we kept silent and waited. The ferret knew what rabbit holes to go into and what ones not to. The ferret chased them out of the holes and you ran and grabbed the net with the rabbit in it. If not, the ferret was just as liable to take the rabbit back into the hole.

Often we used to be snaring rabbits. We were continually snaring, whether it was our own ground or whether it wasn't. Then we'd divide up the spoils and hang them up on a wire up there. You phoned Slaughter, the game merchant, when you had so many and he'd give you your money and that was it. You got more if you'd a hare and if you'd a brown hare they were dearer because they're much bigger and heavier than the white hare – but the white hare makes great soup. There was no myxamatosis in those days and the rabbits used to destroy an awful lot of the crop.

I remember I had snares set up at a fence where I wasn't supposed to be. I had three rabbits and a hare and they're the most awkward things to carry. So I took off my belt and tied them to that and put the belt back on. And dash me I saw a Land Rover coming up the road and I thought: Goodness me, who's that? Then it dawned on me: I wonder if that's the new keeper. Oh no. I saw it turning up there. I undid my belt and let it fall in the heather and I kept walking on. 'Hey! You! Where do you think you're going?' he said. I said: 'I'm just going for a walk.' He said, 'I thought maybe you were poaching.' 'No, I wasn't poaching.' 'Oh, that's different.' So off he went. I'd to turn round and go all the way back and pick up my belt.

We used to look forward to the grouse-shooting season when we went to the beating and I went out with the pony and panniers, to carry back the grouse. The lunch was brought up to the hill when many bottles of whisky were consumed and a good time was had by one and all. The grouse were more plentiful then and a lot of people were employed for the season. We were delighted with our pay at the end of the day. The gamekeeper had a lot of work to do. When he got back to the lodge, he had all the guns to clean ready for the next day, and also to feed all the dogs.

And then the war broke out. I remember we were going to a wedding in 1939 and someone came to the door here and told us to put up black curtains because the war was about to start. We didn't know what to do. We didn't have black curtains. 'Well, you'll have to put up something.' I canna mind what we put up, one of those old rugs I think. So that was the start of it. When the lads were being called up there were a few jobs going and for a while I worked as a postwoman at Dulnain, doing the rounds with the pony.

Then I got a job with the forestry, using one of our horses to drag trees down to the roadside where they could be loaded onto a tractor and cart and taken to the station. The thinner trees were used as pit props, and if they needed bigger stuff they just cut them in 10-foot lengths and you dragged that out. But for the pit props the longer and thinner the tree the better. Our other horse was left on the farm to do the work there, but this one was working in the forestry the whole time. Eventually I got him stabled down at Leantach at the bottom of the road and a retired gamekeeper from Lochindorb would feed him in the morning, so that gave me an extra half-hour at home. I worked there from eight o'clock right on to two and if I managed to drag out enough trees to make about two pounds in money, I could come home then and do the rest of the farm work. If you made two pounds, you were quite happy. There were people there dressing the wood, getting it ready to put on the tractor and trailer. Every stick was counted. There was a 'hooker-on' – an Irishman who used to hook on my drags. You had to provide your own drag chain of course and swingle tree – all your own harness – and when he was attaching your wood to the drag, you were away getting your next tree.

There were Canadians working there and quite a lot of local folk and you knew most of them. Some of them would cycle out from Grantown. There weren't a lot of women at first until the timber corps arrived (They called them the lumber Jills). They stayed at Muckrach Lodge and the lorry picked them up in the morning at eight o'clock. Each one got a different job to do. And then they'd to gather the 'hag' – the branches they cut off the trees – all into rows and that had to be burned.

When I got home I'd to start doing my own jobs. There were always beasts to muck out and what not. During that time Hugh Mathieson moved into Clachbain, the next place up the road, and he used to help out. If he was here he would help with the cattle and if I was over there I would feed his sheep. So it worked both ways, working sort of hand-in-hand. And by that time we'd started using the tractor more than the horses.

Rita joined the Land Army. She was second pair at Tullochgribban, which means she drove the second pair of horses there. And when the crop was in she could go to the wood as well, with their horse, so she didn't have time to work on our farm. After the war she worked as housekeeper in various places and later she became a milk recorder and then she got married.

Betty was doing her war work up where the station used to be. The Army had a shed there where they packed all the Army blankets and tied them up in bundles for going away to different places, herself and another two girls. Later, she worked in Mrs Barclay's shoe shop in Grantown and then in the Tuckshop Tearoom in Carrbridge for many years before she married. She was dux in the school and got all the special prizes, so that's why Mrs Barclay asked her to go and work with her.

So that left me to do the farm work. Our father wasn't fit by then. He was bedridden for many years with arthritis. Our mother looked after the hens and the cows and made the cheese and butter and she was always making oatcakes.

We also had evacuees. People went round and asked if you could take in any evacuees and my Mother took in two girls. She used to write to them afterwards.

The war didn't really make much difference to us. You had your own tatties and eggs and milk and meal. Some people complained about the lack of sugar to make jam, but we always had a lot of honey. We took off our honey in sections and I did it for the neighbour too – Mrs MacDonald up at Rynechra. Once she nearly choked me with sulphur. I was going through this really narrow place, carrying the crate, and she shouted, 'There's a bee in your veil' and started firing the sulphur at me. I couldn't do anything. My hands were full of the honey.

After the war, when my sisters had left home, Jessie Robertson and I used to knock about together. Jessie lived in Dulnain Bridge. Her father was the blacksmith, but Jessie stayed in the old granny's house up at Highfield, up the Skye of Curr road. She was in school with us and we always kept up the friendship.

We went on a lot of holidays together. She couldn't drive but I had a van. We once went for a week's holiday to Uig on Skye. It cost £2 each for bed and board and one and nine for the petrol. Just imagine that! We stayed in a boarding house – there wasn't so much bed and breakfast in those days – and we had plenty food. We enjoyed every minute of it. Of course your holidays are what you make of them.

We joined the Aberdeen-Angus Club. That was our holidays. We used to go away with them every year to farms here and there. We thoroughly enjoyed that. How it started was: There was this traveller here – Bob Smith, he was a traveller for the North-eastern and he stayed in Forres – and he said: 'Why don't you go on those Aberdeen-Angus outings? They're grand outings.' He knew the place they were going to. I said I wouldn't go unless Jessie was going, so I phoned Jessie and she said: 'Oh what do you think MacQueen, will we go?' So I said yes, and that was the start of it.

We went to France, Germany, Italy, Norway, Switzerland and Austria, those kind of places, and where Julie Andrews sang in 'The Sound of Music', we were right up on the hill there, where she stood to sing that song.

I was also in the WRI which I joined in 1937, right out of school. Our mother was president that year and a few of us used to cycle down the road to the meetings. And I went to whist drives and that sort of thing and also on trips with the WRI. Once we were on the banks of the River Elbe in Germany and we were ordered off. A Frau Wittenburg was going to take us through this birch wood where these wagons had been left in wartime. But she wasn't supposed to do that. Of course we went to the banks of the Elbe – I've a photograph of it – and were standing looking out when this hooter noise came from the other side of the river and somebody shouted in German to her; 'Get off there immediately!' That was the time Jessie said to me: 'Do you think we'll be safe on this bus, see where the driver's sitting?' I said: 'I think we'll be safe enough.' It was a left-hand drive you see. Oh what a laugh we had afterwards! Good laughs. Always good laughs

Then Jessie and I joined the Strathspey Farmers' Club. I'd always been involved with the Grantown Show, as had my mother and father. Father received an award when he retired from the club after many years. It was a gold watch and chain. Apart from showing the horses, I used to enter eggs and butter and cheese and stuff like that. I was on the women's committee and the show committee. Jessie was in charge of the women's committee and after her I was in charge of it. Jessie was voted president, in 1971 (the first lady president of the club) and I followed as president, in 1989. Having to make a speech was the worst part. Always before you went to bed the night before, you'd be thinking: 'What have I to say? Who have I to thank?' I'm an honorary president now and still attend every year. This year (2015)

I got a surprise when they asked me to present the prizes in the domestic section.

Another interest I had was in breeding Highland ponies. Back in 1945, when old Tommy our Highland pony was failing, I bought a filly from Lady MacGregor, Upper Stronachan, Argyll. That was the start and then we put it to one of Cameron Ormiston's horses. She had a lovely foal, so we kept that. We had other foals and they were sold eventually, once I had them all quietened down, broken to bridles, that sort of thing. The last one had a foal two years ago. Oh yes, horses were always part of my life.

I still have an old horse collar, a real old-fashioned one, called a storm collar. We had a bonfire over at the old steading there and Rita and me were supposed to burn the collar and I said to Rita, 'I'm going to keep that.' So I sneaked it out and took it down through the broom. A few years back, I took it in here, cleaned it all and took it to Gammack, the saddler in Aberlour and asked him to pad it. It's out in that loft there now, with all sorts of other stuff. There's even the window of an old Model T Ford. You never know when that might come in handy!

All this time I continued to look after the farm. Rita and Betty were married so it was just my mother and me, but Rita would come and look after things when I was off on holiday. Over the years I built up the numbers of cattle from fourteen to twenty – we always kept two heifers. Then I bought an Aberdeen-Angus bull from the Dell of Killiehuntly. He was called McPherson, so we called him Old McPherson. If there was a cow bulling over at Clachbain, he'd be lying in the field and we'd just go out and say to him: 'McPherson. There's a job for you over at Clachbain.' And he would be up on his feet and off over the hill to Clachbain. And then he'd come home, quite easy-oasy. Job done! Where have you been?

I was on the Community Council when it started, with Alec Grant and James Herd the schoolteacher and a few others. There was a good response to it and I was on the Council for a number of years. But we didn't make any really important decisions.

In the dark evenings I kept myself occupied with various hobbies. First I made models of old black houses, like the ones I had seen in Uist when I was a girl. Just after that, I was sitting here one night and I wasn't really interested in what was on TV so I was thinking of something else to do when something caught my eye. The walls in this room were a pale shade of green and I decided to decorate them. First I drew a picture of the hens at that end of the wall, right down to the corner, being chased by the new cockerel that my Mother had, with one hen saying to the other one: 'Slow up a bit. He's going to miss both of us.' Then I did another picture of a lady from the Ferness road who came here with a goose. We already had a goose and a gander. The day after she came we let the goose out with the other one and what did they do? They just took to the air and flew off, away down to Carrbridge. I phoned and told her and she came back, and away at the end of the road she spotted the goose. We had gone down with our bikes, Rita and me. The lady bent down to pick up the goose and it just took to the air again. Away she went, away back to the Ferness road again, so we left her. By that time our old goose was at the conking-out stage and she did. So here's the old gander left without a wife so I made an artificial goose with a bag and tied it with a long string. He started dragging it about and he would trail it right down to the burn and leave it on the side while he went swimming in the burn, then he would come back to it, pick up the string and trail it back up to the house. That was his wife now and you daren't take it off him.

The next drawing was of Mrs Smith, who used to live at Uislich behind Loch Pityoulish, pushing her son Donnie in a peat barrow to take him to Kincardine Church to get christened. He was five years old by then. That was Donnie Smith, who used to farm at Lurg, Nethy Bridge. I drew Loch Pityoulish and the wee church and all the folk that were there. I used oil paints and they came out very well on top of the house paint. I also did a picture of George Rafferty, the former vet, sitting in a chair here, and one of my sister Betty going down the brae on a pushbike and she couldn't find the brakes and she was shouting and bawling.

When the minister came to visit once he asked me to explain all the pictures, but I told him some of them weren't suitable for a minister. There were some I had to scratch out too when members of people's families came visiting. My Mother didn't mind them but my sister Rita thought they were terrible. When I had to go into hospital, Rita said: 'You'll notice a change when you get home.' She'd had the place all decorated and covered up all the pictures. But they're still there, underneath!

PART 3

Looking Back

I've seen many changes in my life but the main one is the loss of all the little farms and crofts in the glen. When I think now on the number of ruins around the hill and I've had tea in every one of them. The steading's down at Rynechra now and I've had my tea in that house, down to Sleuch, I've had my tea there, and a housie half-way down where there was a man MacDonald – the house didn't have a name – I've had my tea in there. And coming back down the hill to Rychraggan, I've had my tea there too. At Rychraggan there was a topper of a well at the bottom of the field and the old lady lost her wedding ring in it. Many folk used to go there looking for the ring – but they never found it. Back down again to Tilly High (Upper Tullochgribban), then right down, follow the burn to Cairnloch, had my tea in there, also at Rynruich and Coul-na-Moul and Green Gutter, just down from Achnahannet, where my two old aunties used to live. Rita and I both went for our tea there and we had our own special mugs which they kept just for us. Now there's nobody left in any of those houses. Just ruins.

I've seen lots and lots of changes in farming, from the times when the cattle were all tied inside the byre in the winter time and you carried their feed all the way from the barn to the byre and as often as not you'd lose half of it as it would be blown off the fork. Then the cows would get out to the water in the middle of the day and while they were out you'd be putting the turnips into the trough, so many neeps each, then they would come tearing back, barging in the door and everybody went to their own stall without any bother at all and they were all tied by chain. Once they were all outside, usually not until about June, you started mucking out the sheds and the loose boxes where the stirks were kept. It was all done by hand with the graip and the shovel and the big brush for brushing the causey. Nowadays none of that goes on. Nobody uses a graip now. It's all big diggers and big tractors. We had the wee tractors, first the one with the cleat wheels, then the old Fergie. It was hardy. We used to go up to the peat moss with that. You couldn't take a big tractor to the peat moss. It'd sink out of sight!

After all the other jobs were done you'd to scrape all the dung off the carts and paint them. You did that every year. You'd a thing for taking off the wheel – a wooden jack kind of thing with a chain on it and you hooked the chain on to the spring below. That lifted off the wheel and you were able to pull it out a wee bit and you greased the wheel then put it back on and let the wheels down again. We used to like getting that job to do.

The ploughing and harrowing, all that was done by the horses and you should have seen the speed the horses would go when they saw our mother coming to the field with the tea because they knew fine they would be getting a piece too.

Oh aye there's a lot of changes. The implements started getting bigger and bigger, things that you couldn't use in those days because the fields were so small, there were fences everywhere. Then the binder came in and the mower too. A lot of people changed their mower from the old-fashioned one with the pole that was pulled by the horses to one with a short pole that was pulled by a tractor. With the older tractors, the exhaust was coming out the bottom and if you were sitting on the seat on the mower, it would nearly choke you. Eventually they put the exhaust higher up, so that was much better. Combine harvesters started to come in after that. The small crofters and farmers couldn't afford them so they got contractors in. The combines are huge now too.

The breeds of cattle have all changed. Firstly there was Aberdeen-Angus and then the Shorthorn came in, followed by the Herefords and then the Continentals. We had one Limousin latterly, but the rest were just the ordinary cows. The milkers were just dairy cows, I don't know what breed. We had one that came out of Dalbuiack. She was white and we called her Snowdrop. We had another one that was blue-grey with black teats. She was a right good milker. You could milk her outside.

When the men were at the hoe, hoeing turnips, there might be up to a dozen of them working together. It was quite common if you wanted someone to do something for you to say, 'I'll give you a day at the hoe in return.' They were very particular about the rows being neat. Rita and I would be out on the bikes and when we got home we would say, 'What straight turnip drills we saw in such and such a place.' We don't see that any more, as the seeds are all broadcast and then the turnips are grazed in the field.

And the sawmills, that's another change. Every place had its own sawmill for their fence posts and so on. Now you have to get them all sent from Inverness.

Out on the hill, there's a lot more heather-burning done now. Away back they used to let it grow and grow. When they had a fire it would get out of control and the whole hill would be burned. It's far better now.

When I walked every day to the school at Dulnain Bridge and back, I must have noted all the places of interest en route and taken note of all the history handed down from my parents. One road from the village led up to Finlarig, which takes its name from the limestone quarries. It was also called the Holy Pass. Very little is now left to mark the old chapel yard at Finlarig. The last man to be buried there was an Indian servant who accompanied his master to Strathspey. The road leads on to Balnouchk, 'the crest of the hill', from where we look down on Achnahannet, 'field of the holy site'. We can see the last remaining wall of Green Gutter where my two old aunties lived into their nineties. The reason Green Gutter got its name was that there was a well out in front of it and the water was bubbling up all the time so it went right round the front of the house and kept everything green. When the old ladies died, the staircase was taken out of the house and put into the cottage round the back of my house. Mary and Jane were the names of the old aunties – one was stout and one was thin – and when the older one got ill, she was taken down here in the cart.

We can see the old Church of Duthil, the burying place of the chiefs of Clan Grant. The last to be buried in the mausoleum there was Ian Charles, Earl of Seafield, who died in 1881. The coffin was borne there by a number of clansmen and placed on a trestle beside his father, the door being closed for the last time. The mausoleum was designed by William Playfair and it is said that when the doors were closed for the last time, the keys were thrown into the Spey.

Wending my way down the hill, I used to hear the noise and splash of the big wheel that drove the threshing mill. The dam was at the roadside and when the sluice gates were opened the force of water drove the mill. The sheep fank was close by and the dipper, conveniently sited beside the dam. All long since gone.

As I come back up the hill towards home, I pass Lower Achnahannet where the road used to cross a ford just before the brae going up to the steading. I can still remember the shape and size of each stepping stone. Over the years a bridge was built and then a cattle grid. In my young days the elderly couple who stayed there were Grants, known to us as 'Ma and Da'. They used to have what in those days were known as 'Glasgow loons' who helped with all the duties, inside and out. These boys were very ignorant of country life, but Da coached them well. They slept in a lean-to at the back of the house and had their own entrance. Ma also had a girl working in the house who was known as 'Mary Slow Motion' and they were all one big happy family.

Just below Achnahannet was Annie Fraser's croft, which had a box bed in the kitchen and another bed in the sitting-room for Annie's brother who was a piper. Annie was the boss. She kept a few cows and quite a few hens. When the brother died, all sorts of stories went around about a piper playing at midnight so many curious people would come and listen for a tune. Annie employed many boys at different times, especially for the peat-cutting. It was the done thing for farm workers to write a comment on the back of the stable or byre door, very often not in favour of the boss. In this case one of them advised against feeing for Annie Fraser, as she had 'a tongue that would clip cloots'. Annie walked across to the Achnahannet road every Tuesday to meet the grocer, Henry Surtees from Grantown, who came in his pony and trap. She brought eggs to sell and usually had enough almost to cover the cost of her messages.

Walking on down the hill I am now in full view of Mullinfenechan, the mill that served the local farms with oatmeal. I pass Balnaan, 'farm of the ford', and look across at ancient Muckrach Castle, and reach my journey's end, right at the door of the old smiddy where the path leads over the hill and back home.

How sad it is seeing all the old buildings disappearing. During the heather-burning season, one comes across the remains of these places with paths still visible to small patches of ground which had been broken up by the spade, stones carried off the fields still there in small piles where now bracken is taking over. Many of the roads between the crofts are now overgrown. The croft at Cairnloch used to have cobble stones still quite visible round the front of the old steading and a rowan tree grew in the corner of what would have been the garden. Most of the crofts had rowan trees. One old tree had a huge split in the bark and a swarm of bees made their home there, so the tree was oozing with honey.

On this hillside one old lady told me that eleven chimneys smoked each day. Now there are none. The names I remember are Drumroy, Anaboard, Ryluchrach, Corrycharcle, Ryndean and Glencharrach.

Easter Rynechra, up at the top of the hill, was very isolated. The means of communication was to hang a white sheet on the garden fence so we knew there was a message. The washing was always done outside. An old iron boiler stood in a stone fireplace near the well, which saved carting water from the house. Many a day when it was stormy the old lady could not get to the well so buckets of snow were brought in and left to melt. In earlier days the cows had restricted grazing so they were tethered and moved to a fresh stance every day. Mrs MacDonald kept a good few hives of bees and did very well on heather honey as during the shooting season members of the party would stop to buy a few sections.

The slates on the roof at East Rynechra are great big thick ones which are supposed to have come from the church at Duthil. They were carted up to Rynechra before World War I along an old track which can still be followed on the moor. Before that it was turf roofs which caused a lot of dust but were easily replaced. A lot of the houses used to be bad for the smoke with the peat reek stinging the eyes and leaving colourful streaks on the walls. One man who paid a visit to the house one evening said he had been there half an hour before he saw a wifie sitting in the corner, the smoke was so bad. The old lady slept in a box bed in the kitchen with double doors closing in the middle, which must have been very warm in the winter. A brick was left by the fireside all day and put into the bed at night to warm it.

One wonders how they all survived in these crofts on the hillside with so little fertile land, but the old folk were pretty much self-sufficient. They'd be pickling the eggs and salting the mutton. There were always two big earthenware jars of pickled eggs in the press and that was to use for your baking and everything while the hens weren't laying. Same with the herring. The boys would come round with the herring and you would salt them and keep them in a wee barrel. My Mother did all these things and I pickled eggs myself.

There were also plenty of rabbits and hares to eke things out. Quite a lot of time was spent making new snare pins. The big pin was the one that held the rope and the snare attached and the smaller pin, the 'star pin', was set at a particular height depending on whether it was intended for rabbits or hares. There was a hare drive every year in December. I have a photo of one up at Balnouchk with my mother going up with a big basket of pieces (food) for the men. All the neighbours would meet at an appointed place and line up from there. The shoot was always very successful and the hares and rabbits would be handed over to friends and neighbours at the end of it. Then the organiser produced a dram, which was enjoyed by one and all.

Most of the crofts had a place built to burn lime. Stones were crushed and burnt there and the grit and ash were spread on the field.

I gave up farming bit by bit as I grew older, but I still have my hens. There are sheep around in the winter, as Neil Gordon puts up his wintering hoggs, but there's no cattle this side of the grid. I also still have the little cottage down the back, which the shooters use as a lunch hut.

It's fine and free. Just myself and the hens and the cat. That's all. The hens keep me going. I like to go out and feed them and look for their eggs, even though my eyesight isn't very good and I have to use a frame for walking. Last week there was a hen turned up with nine chickens, then one with five, one with six and one with four. All in the one week. With me losing my eyesight, I couldn't see where they were laying, so I asked the gamekeeper to go and have a rake round. Right enough he found four different nests and he told me about this hen sitting under the old cart in the yard. That was the one that came home with nine chickens. I know them all individually and even that rabbit – a wild rabbit there – he walks under the cart and if I put a dish of flaked maize out, he knows some of it will fall out so he eats that. He walks in front of me, then behind me there's the hen with the six chickens and then another chicken flies up on my shoulder and sits there. I heard a voice one day saying: 'Careful Madge, you're speeding.' It was the boss of the shooting here. 'What a menagerie!' he said, and I suppose it's a comical sight for anyone who comes visiting.

I'm up at six thirty every morning and I go to bed any time after ten and in between those times I'm reading or drawing or writing or falling asleep and the paper falling on the floor. And answering phone calls and feeding the hens, even in my sleep, wondering where such and such a hen is laying. I feed them twice a day and there's four that come to the door every night at nine for a piece.

I have visitors every other day, about fifteen a week. There are people who have been coming for years, since our grandfather's day, generation after generation, and there are my nieces and nephews and their families. Then there are people who want to find out about where their relatives lived in the past.

I'm glad I lived the life I did. I wouldn't have wanted it any different. I never wanted to get married or have children. That was the furthest from my thoughts. My father was an invalid for fourteen years and then my mother took ill with arthritis as well. I just considered it was my job to look after them. Oh aye, I was quite happy. As I say: eat, drink and be merry, that's me!